200
Capture Mates

200
Capture Mates

Fred Wilson
&
Bruce Alberston

Cardoza Publishing

Cardoza Publishing is the foremost gaming publisher in the world, with a library of over 200 up-to-date and easy-to-read books and strategies. These authoritative works are written by the top experts in their fields and with more than 9,500,000 books in print, represent the best selling and most popular gaming books anywhere.

1ST EDITION

Copyright © 2007 by Fred Wilson & Bruce Alberston
- All Rights Reserved -

Library of Congress Catalog Card No: 2007926508
ISBN: 1-58042-215-2

Visit our web site—www.cardozapub.com—or write for a full list of books and computer strategies.

CARDOZA PUBLISHING
P.O. Box 1500, Cooper Station, New York, NY 10276
Phone (800) 577-WINS
email: cardozapub@aol.com
www.cardozapub.com

Contents

ABOUT THE AUTHORS

Fred Wilson, the owner of Fred Wilson Chess Books in New York City, is among the finest chess teachers and authors. He is the author of *A Picture History of Chess* and *101 Questions on How to Play Chess*. Life Master Bruce Alberston is a well-known teacher and trainer in New York. He's written and narrated the CD-Rom, *Quick Kills on the Chessboard* and is the author of *51 Chess Openings for Beginners, 217 Chess Opening Traps* (both for Cardoza Publishing) and the bestselling *Chess Mazes*.

For Cardoza Publishing, Wilson and Alberston have collaborated on *202 Surprising Mates, 303 Tricky Chess Tactics, 303 Tricky Checkmates, 303 Tricky Chess Puzzles, 303 More Tricky Chess Puzzles, 202 Checkmates for Children* and *200 Capture Mates*.

Introduction

This book is a great learning tool that challenges you to solve puzzles and find the mates in 200 unique and fun checkmating situations. You'll be using capture mates—a chess term for taking an opponent's piece and winning at the same time—to accomplish each of these victories.

The first 100 of these puzzles are one move mates. Find the right capture, checkmate the king, and you win! The second 100 puzzles are more challenging; these are two move mates. You make a move that captures a piece, your opponent makes a forced reply, and then you swoop in for the kill. Of course, at the end, we provide you with solutions for all the puzzles, though hopefully, you'll get most of them without our help!

Our puzzles teach you to use every piece to find the mates. To keep the puzzles interesting, we've tossed in a few tricky mates as well! But can you solve them?

Get ready for some fun, and on the way, learn how to checkmate your opponent and be a better chess player!

Keys for Chess Notation

This section is to get you more familiar with chess notation so the answers in the back of the book don't look like gobbledygook. In the next chapter, we're going to run through a short game played by one of the authors. Try to follow the notation as the moves are presented. We'll give a diagram after several moves so you can check yourself. Refer to the key below for any help with notation.

K or ♔	stands for king
Q or ♕	stands for queen
R or ♖	stands for rook
B or ♗	stands for bishop
N or ♘	stands for knight
P or ♙	stands for pawn although in practice the "P" is rarely used.
+	Check
#	Checkmate
0-0	Castle kingside
0-0-0	Castle queenside
x	Capture
!	Good move
?	Bad move

Remember, when indicating a capture, you write the square you are making the capture on, rather than the piece you are capturing. We no longer use the symbol P for pawn. A pawn move is indicated by a **lower-case letter,** which identifies the file of the moving pawn.

♞♛ Capture Mates

A **capture mate** is the chess term for taking an enemy man and checkmating the opposing king in the same move. These two concepts—capturing and mating—are the two most important things a player does during a game so it makes a lot of sense to practice both often!

To begin, lets first consider the matter of check, and see how the king gets out of danger.

Diagram A

White is in check from the rook. The rules say he must drop everything he's doing and save his king—in other words, get out of check. There are three methods he can use.

1. Capture

He can **capture** the enemy rook with his bishop, **Bxe8**. Knocking the rook off the board certainly saves his king.

2. Block

He can **block** the check by interposing the bishop between the rook and king, **Be2**.

3. Move

He can **move** his king off the attacking line, **Kd1** (or **d2**, **f1**, **f2**). But not **Ke2**, which is illegal because the king would still be in check.

If the king is unable to get out of check using one of the three methods (capture, block or move), then it's a checkmate and the game is over. Diagram B shows the White king in checkmate.

Diagram B

To turn diagram B into a capture mate we arrange for the Black rook to come to **e8** while taking a White unit. Diagram C shows how.

Diagram C

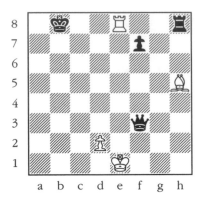

All four Black units—king, queen, rook and pawn—are under fire. But the simple **...Rxe8** is a checkmate (**x** mean takes). In fact, it is a capture mate since Black is capturing an enemy piece *while* mating the king.

The convention in most chess books is to set up positions so that White is to move and give mate. That's because White goes first in a chess game. We can do that simply by reversing the colors and rotating the board.

Diagram D
White Mates In One

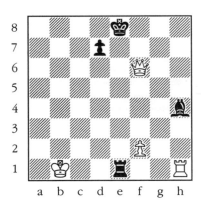

The solution to the problem is **Rxe1 mate**.
To set up a capture mate in two moves, we merely arrange for White to capture twice in forcing the mate.

Diagram E
White Mates in Two

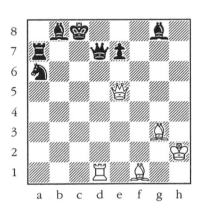

First, White takes the knight at **a6** checking, **1. Bxa6+** (**+** means check), and then, no matter what Black plays, comes the second capture, this time of a bishop, **2. Qxb8#** (**#** is the symbol for mate).

These are composed positions, and there is something artificial about them. Naturally, the reader has a certain right to be skeptical and ask, "Do capture mates come up in real chess games?" The answer is a resounding, "Yes, they do!"

And to prove our case we take a familiar position, the Scholar's Mate.

Diagram F

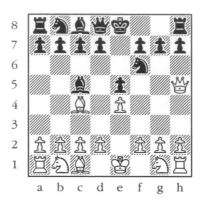

The moves leading up to the diagram are: **1. e4 e5 2. Bc4 Bc5 3. Qh5 Nf6??** We'll simply note that Black's last move was a terrible mistake and that 3 …Qe7 or 3…Qf6 would have been correct.

White wins the game by capturing Black's pawn on f7, checkmating the king as he does so, by **4. Qxf7#**.

Diagram G

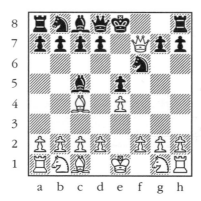

Yes, the most frequently occurring mate also happens to be a capture mate. And while we're still on the Scholar's Mate, here is another version. The moves are: **1. e4 e5 2. Bc4 Bc5 3. Qf3 Nh6? 4. d4 Bxd4.**

Diagram H

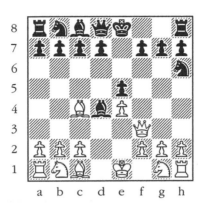

5. Bxh6 removes the defending knight and when Black recaptures, **5...gxh6??** (he should castle instead), White finishes him off with **6. Qxf7#**.

Note that to achieve this White played two consecutive captures. (Always look at all your checks and captures!) And although it looks like a capture mate in two it is not strictly forced. Recall that Black could have castled and stopped the mate. That's one of the differences between actual play and composed problems. The composer can shape the position so that things come out just the way he wants them to.

Still, sometimes the two converge and we have a blend of practical, theoretical, and with luck, the aesthetic.

Our next example, is a version of the Fool's Mate which began, **1. f4 e5 2. fxe5 d6 3. exd6 Bxd6 4. g3 Qg5 5. Nf3??** White should have played 5. Bg2. He didn't, so now he runs into a forced capture mate in two.

Diagram I
Black Mates in Two Moves

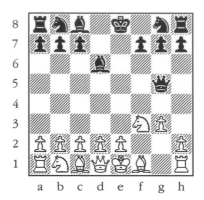

Hope you saw the finale, **5...Bxg3+ 6. hxg3 Qxg3#**. If you're feeling brilliant, you can also start with **5...Qxg3+**, etc.

But you get the idea. Capture mates really do occur in practice. They can happen right out of the opening and they're not so rare as you might at first suppose.

CAPTURES IN GENERAL

We've talked about checkmate, so what about captures? Frankly, you could write several books on capturing. There are gobs of classifications and tons of examples for each.

Let's stand back a little and see if we can keep things comprehensible. We start by observing that the main reason for capturing enemy pieces is to win material and get the larger army.

The standard scenario tells us that the larger army usually wins. The side with the material advantage gets to call the shots, be the attacker and force his opponent to resort to a thankless defense. He eventually breaks down under superior force and the larger army wins.

Are there exceptions to this general rule? Yes. About 1 in a 100. It's the 1% that ends up in the chess books (this one included). The other 99 times, material superiority triumphs, even if it doesn't get recorded for posterity. That's why you take material when you get the opportunity. The odds get stacked in your favor.

In capture mates, the reason for taking material becomes narrowed. The focus is the enemy king and we want to finish him off as quickly as possible! If an opposing piece or two stands in our way, we just remove it from the board to get at the king. There's nothing fancy about our motives or our methods. We take things so we can mate.

The final example is taken from a tournament game between two strong amateurs. It's more about capturing than it is about capture mates, but, of course, mate enters the picture as well.

It's just a position Fred happened to spot when he was strolling by at the World Open Chess Tournament in Philadelphia a few years ago.

Diagram J

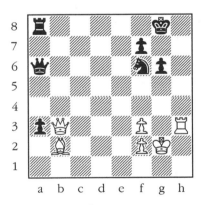

White to play and take something. He rejected 1. Bxa3 Qxa3 2. Qxa3 Rxa3 as it loses a piece. Presumably 1. Qxa3 was rejected for the same reason. So he went for **1. Bxf6**, threatening 2. Rh8#.

But after **1...Qxf6**, White was at a loss for what to do. Probably he realized Black's dangerous advanced a-pawn would now be unstoppable. He tried **2. Qb7 Rd8 3. Rh1 a2 4. Qa7**, but it wasn't good enough because his king came under attack after **4...Qg5+ 5. Kh2** (if 5. Kf1 Rd1+ 6. Ke2 Qd2#) **5...Kg7**, threatening 6...Rh8#. At this point, seeing no defense, White resigned. Of course, he could have tried to bluff his opponent by quickly playing 6. Qd4+?!—all's fair in love, war and chess—but evidently his sense of sportsmanship was too strong to consider this last cheap trick!

Diagram K, after 5...Kg7

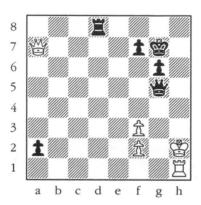

At any rate, what Fred had spotted out of the corner of his eye was that White could have won by playing **1. Qxa3! Qxa3 2. Bxf6** and mate by **Rh8** is imminent.

Diagram L, after 2. Bxf6

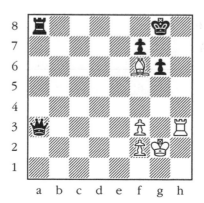

The only way to resist is for Black to return material by **2...Qxf3+ 3. Kxf3 Ra3+ 4. Kg2 Rxh3 5. Kxh3**. But the resulting endgame will be won by White; he has an extra bishop.

So, what's the moral of the story? Mainly, that it's not enough just to see captures; you have to see the right captures! You could also say that Fred sees more out of the corner of his eye than two amateur players staring at the board. But that's why Fred is a Master and the other two are not.

There are several reasons you will not find positions of this type in the main body of the book. First, there is no forced mate in the position, and second, where mate does occur, it does not involve captures. All of this brings us to the...

RULES FOR CAPTURE MATES

Rule Number One

It is always White to move and mate.

Rule Number Two

You can't take more than the stipulated number of moves to solve the problem. If it's White to mate in one, you've got to do it on your very next move. Checkmating in two moves doesn't cut it. And if it's White to mate in two, you've got two moves to work with, not three.

Rules Number Three

White must capture something every time he makes a move. That's the distinguishing feature of capture mates. It means that White may not play a move that doesn't capture a Black unit!

If it's mate in one then White's first and only move must combine capture and checkmate. If it's mate in two, White's first move must be a capture, and his second move must also be a capture combined with checkmate. Black's move can be any legal move, capture or non-capture.

Rule Number Four

Okay, there is no rule number four! It stops at three. But we strongly suggest that you solve the problems in your head without the aid of outside devices. If you feel that setting up the position on a chessboard will help, then do so, but once you've got it set up, don't touch the pieces. Solve it in your head.

When you think you've got it, jot down your answer in chess notation and check it against the solutions in the back of the book. For complete beginners, who may be a little "shaky" at reading and writing chess notation, we have also provided *answer diagrams*, although for the mates in two moves we only show an *answer diagram* for the final, checkmating position.

That's it. The rest is up to you. So get cracking and go to work. Solve some capture mates!

White to Play and Mate in One Move

PROBLEMS 1 TO 100

You know what you have to do here, checkmate the Black king in one move. And you have to do it while taking something. You'll find a whole array of captures by the queen, rook, bishop, knight, pawn, and king. So, don't get sidetracked. You're after the one capture that administers the checkmate.

You're well aware that a king cannot approach his counterpart and attack him directly. Nevertheless, a king can give checkmate by moving off an attacking line and unmasking a piece in the rear. It's the stationary piece in the rear—queen, rook, or bishop—one that moves in a direct line, that gives the checkmate. It cannot be a knight or pawn. We call this a **discover checkmate**. Watch for it.

Also keep a lookout for pawn mates. Remember that a pawn upon reaching the 8th rank can promote to a queen. It can also underpromote to a lesser piece. We've slipped in a few of those as well. Our dirty tricks department insisted that we put in an *en passant* mate, so we did that too. If you don't know what *en passant* is, you'd better check it out, it's part of the rules.

White to Move
1.

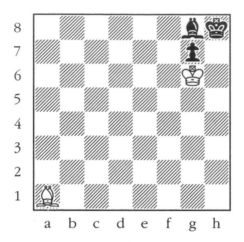

White to Move
2.

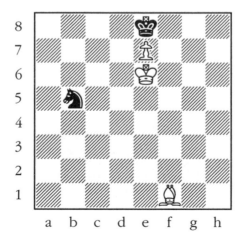

White to Move
3.

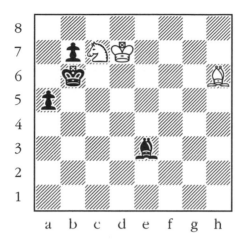

White to Move
4.

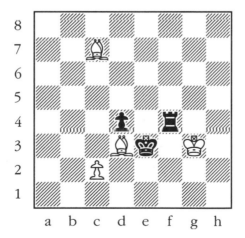

White to Move
5.

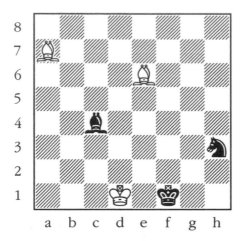

White to Move
6.

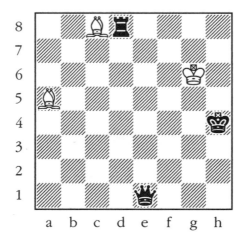

White to Move
7.

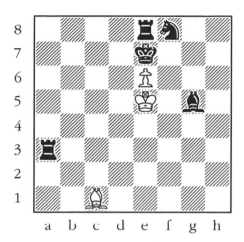

White to Move
8.

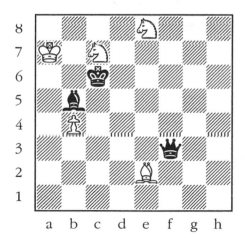

White to Move
9.

White to Move
10.

White to Move
11.

White to Move
12.

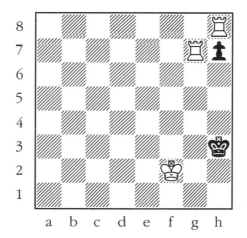

White to Move
13.

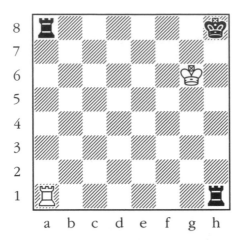

White to Move
14.

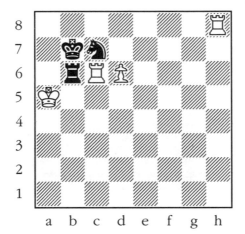

White to Move
15.

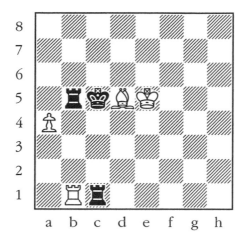

White to Move
16.

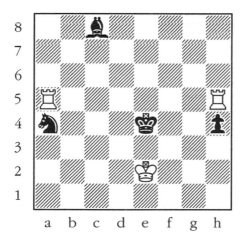

White to Move
17.

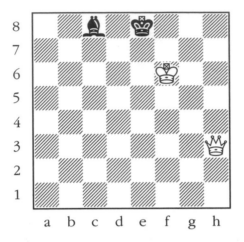

White to Move
18.

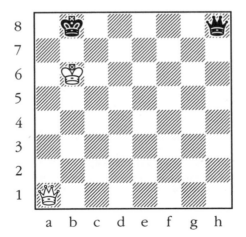

White to Move
19.

White to Move
20.

White to Move
21.

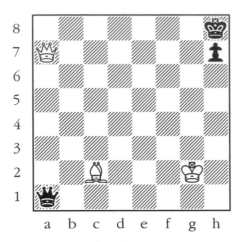

White to Move
22.

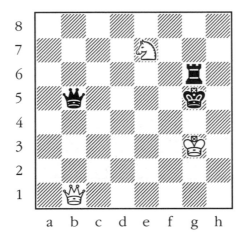

White to Move
23.

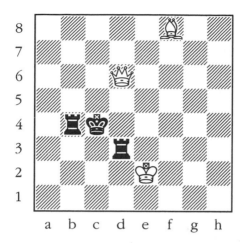

White to Move
24.

White to Move
25.

White to Move
26.

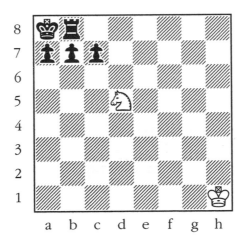

White to Move
27.

White to Move
28.

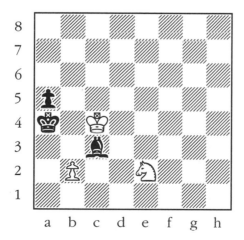

White to Move
29.

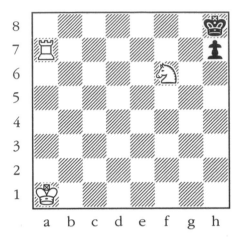

White to Move
30.

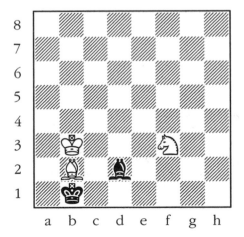

White to Move
31.

White to Move
32.

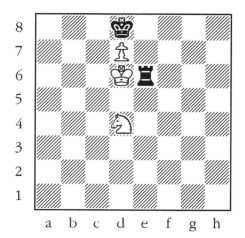

White to Move
33.

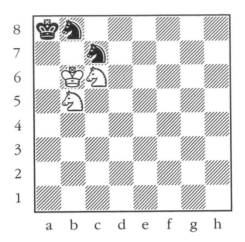

White to Move
34.

White to Move
35.

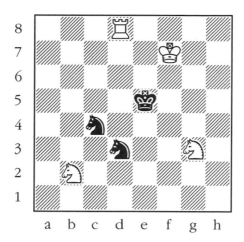

White to Move
36.

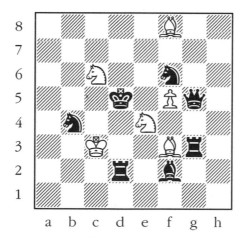

White to Move
37.

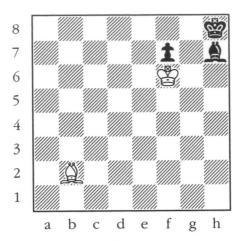

White to Move
38.

White to Move
39.

White to Move
40.

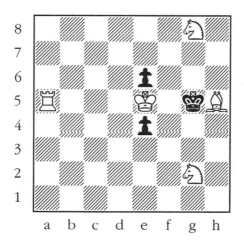

White to Move
41.

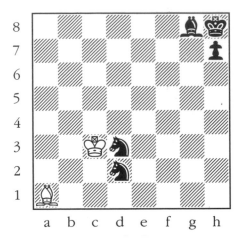

White to Move
42.

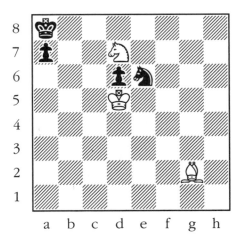

White to Move
43.

White to Move
44.

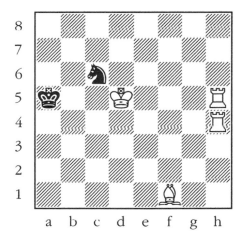

White to Move
45.

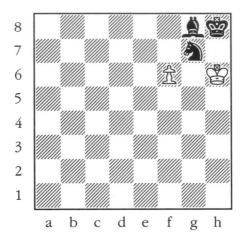

White to Move
46.

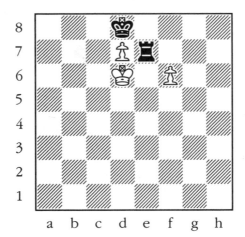

White to Move
47.

White to Move
48.

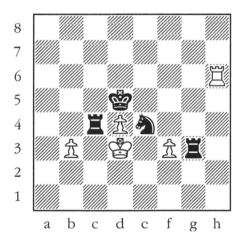

White to Move
49.

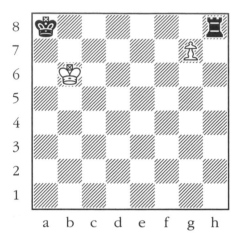

White to Move
50.

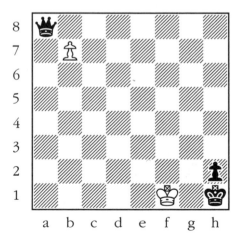

White to Move
51.

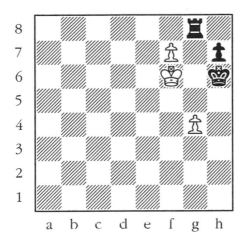

White to Move
52.

White to Move
53.

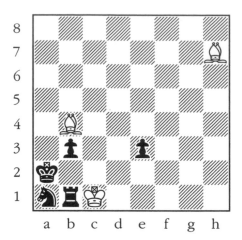

White to Move
54.

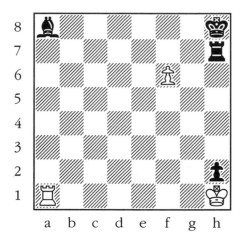

White to Move
55.

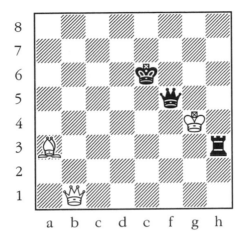

White to Move
56.

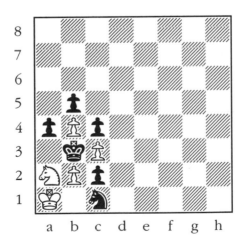

White to Move
57.

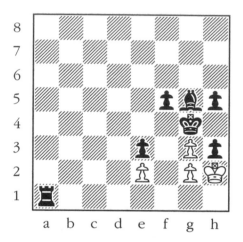

White to Move
58.

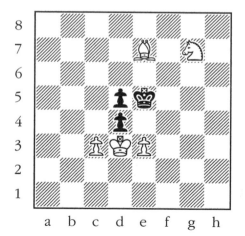

White to Move
59.

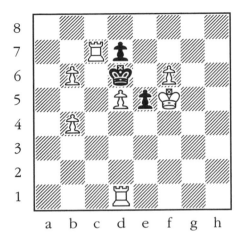

White to Move
60.

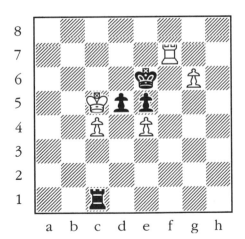

White to Move
61.

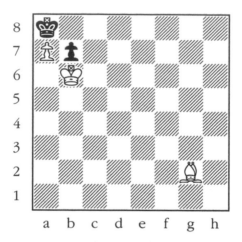

White to Move
62.

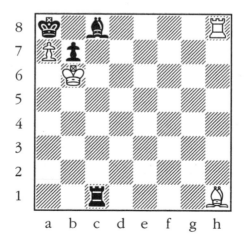

White to Move
63.

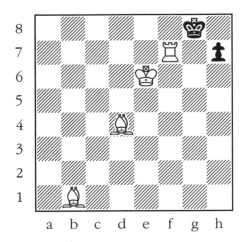

White to Move
64.

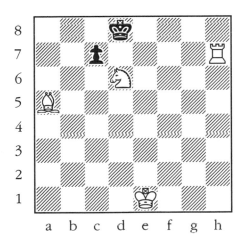

White to Move
65.

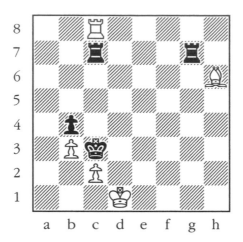

White to Move
66.

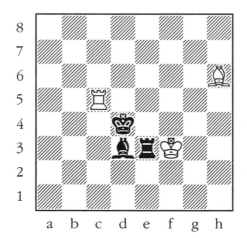

White to Move
67.

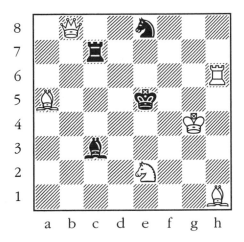

White to Move
68.

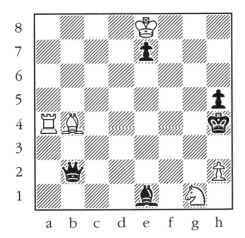

White to Move
69.

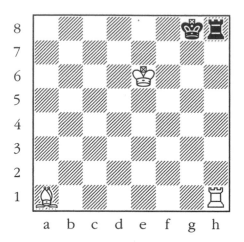

White to Move
70.

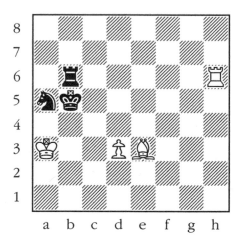

White to Move
71.

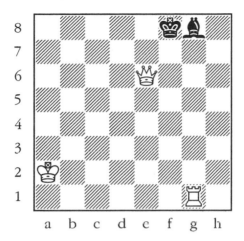

White to Move
72.

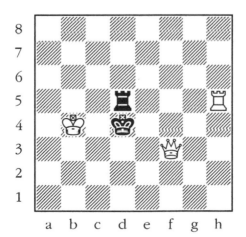

White to Move
73.

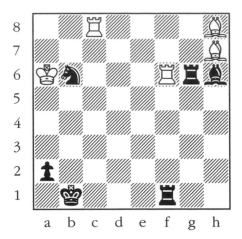

White to Move
74.

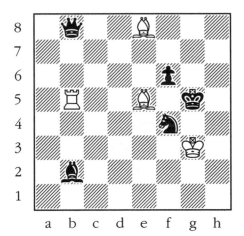

White to Move
75.

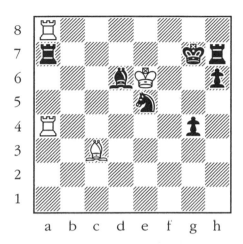

White to Move
76.

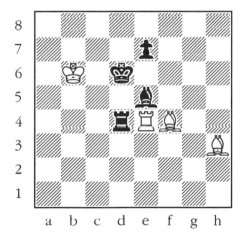

White to Move
77.

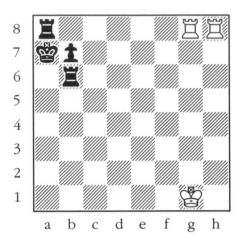

White to Move
78.

White to Move
79.

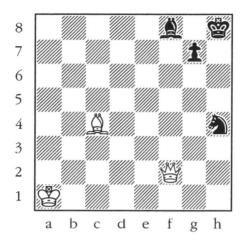

White to Move
80.

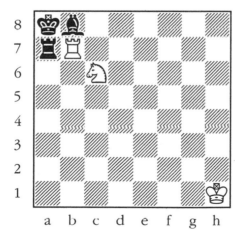

White to Move
81.

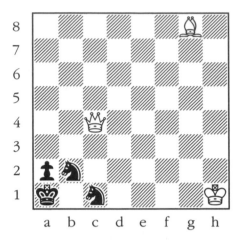

White to Move
82.

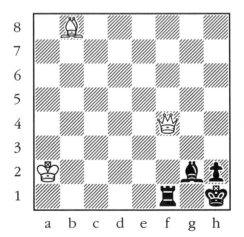

White to Move
83.

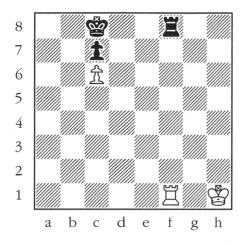

White to Move
84.

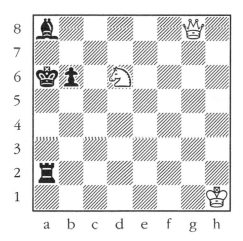

White to Move
85.

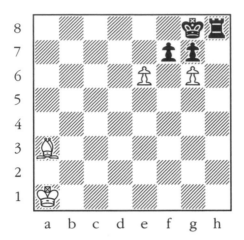

White to Move
86.

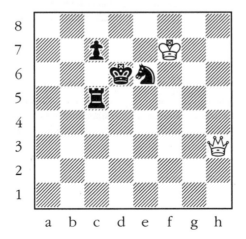

White to Move
87.

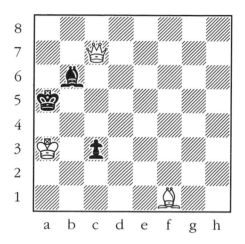

White to Move
88.

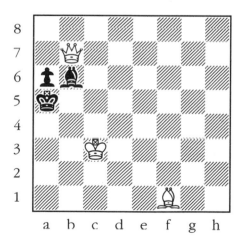

White to Move
89.

White to Move
90.

White to Move
91.

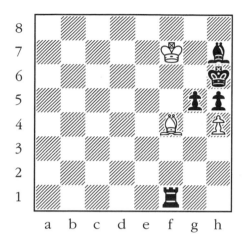

White to Move
92.

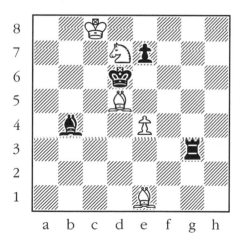

White to Move
93.

White to Move
94.

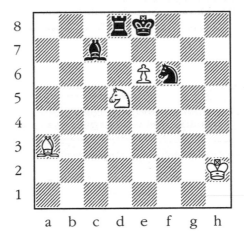

White to Move
95.

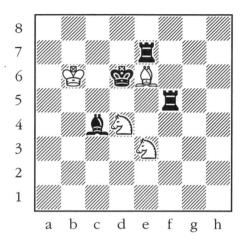

White to Move
96.

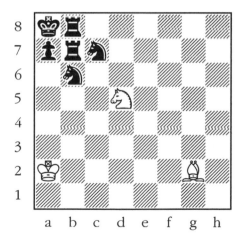

White to Move
97.

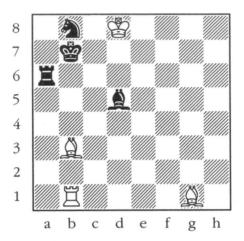

White to Move
98.

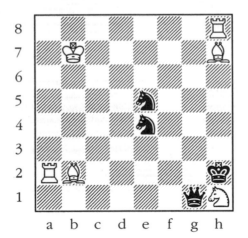

White to Move
99.

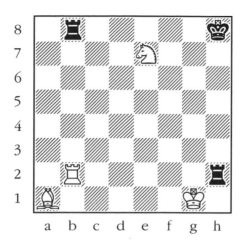

White to Move
100.

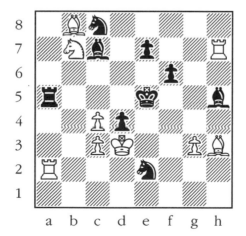

♞♛ White to Play and Mate in Two Moves

PROBLEMS 101 TO 200

Having come this far you can consider the first 100 problems as warm ups for the harder stuff in this chapter, mate in two. That means you have to see three ply ahead; a White move, a Black response, and a second White move delivering checkmate. And you know that all the White moves have to be captures.

It's going to require both seeing and visualization skills. The seeing skills you already acquired in the previous chapter where you had to see the capture mate that was sitting on the board directly in front of you.

This chapter is where you acquire the visualization skills. You're going to have to picture positions in your head that have not yet appeared on the board. Fortunately, while the positions are off in the future, it is the not too distant future. So they should be within your reach.

By the time you finish this chapter, we expect your chess strength to have increased at least one class. You'll be on the lookout for captures the instant they arise on the board. And you'll be familiar with many of the standard checkmating patterns. You'll have developed that intuitive sense for when the enemy king is vulnerable and when your pieces can bore in for the mate.

White to Move
101.

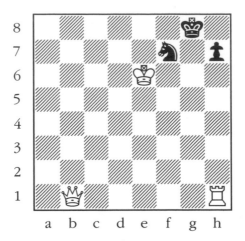

White to Move
102.

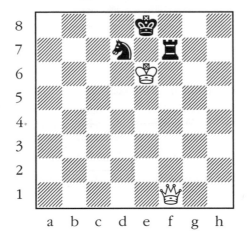

White to Move
103.

White to Move
104.

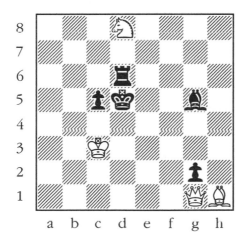

White to Move
105.

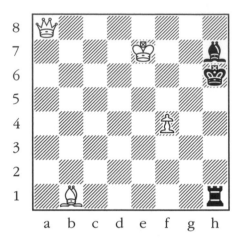

White to Move
106.

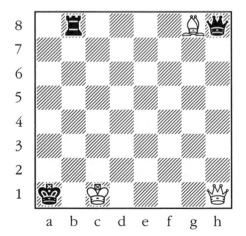

White to Move
107.

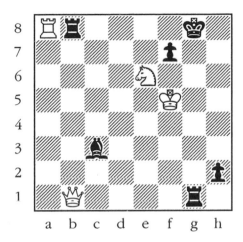

White to Move
108.

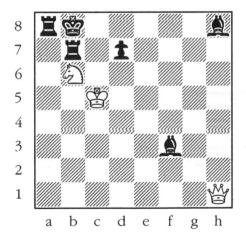

White to Move
109.

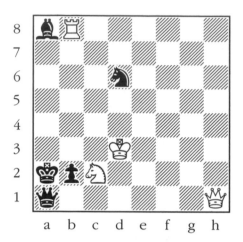

White to Move
110.

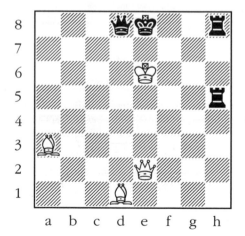

White to Move
111.

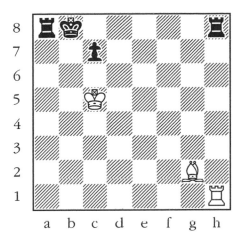

White to Move
112.

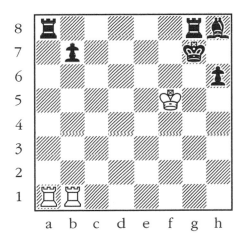

White to Move
113.

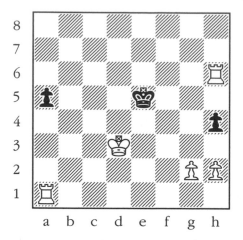

White to Move
114.

White to Move
115.

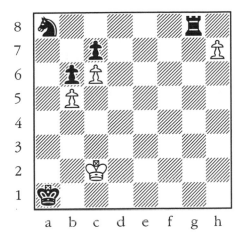

White to Move
116.

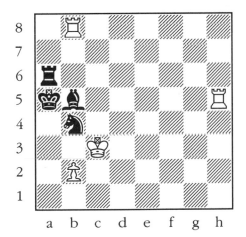

White to Move
117.

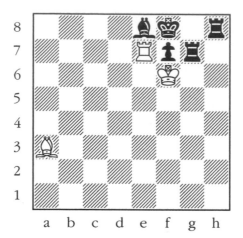

White to Move
118.

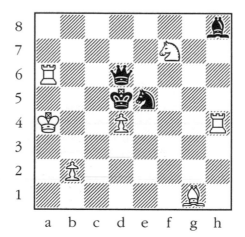

White to Move
119.

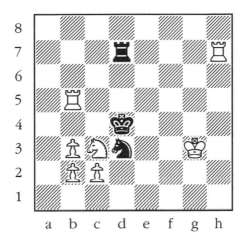

White to Move
120.

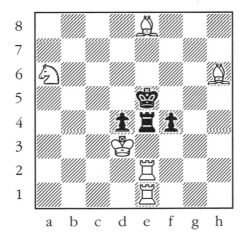

White to Move
121.

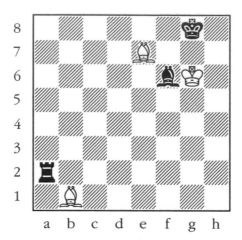

White to Move
122.

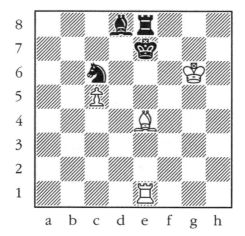

White to Move
123.

White to Move
124.

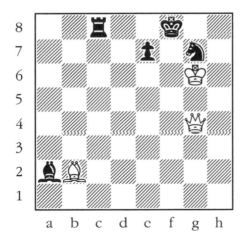

White to Move
125.

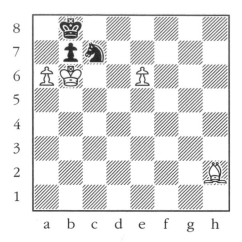

White to Move
126.

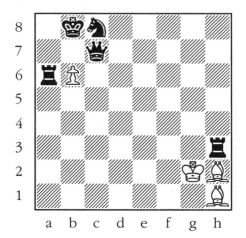

White to Move
127.

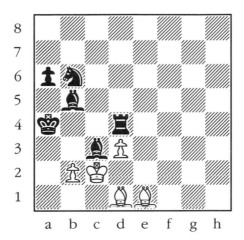

White to Move
128.

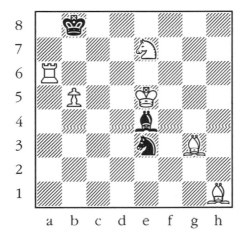

White to Move
129.

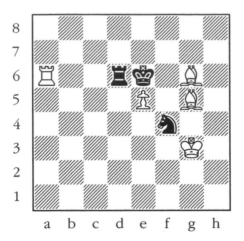

White to Move
130.

White to Move
131.

White to Move
132.

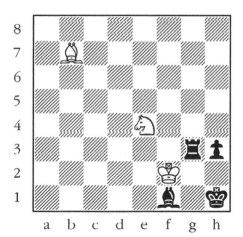

White to Move
133.

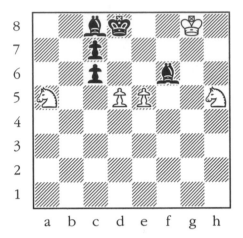

White to Move
134.

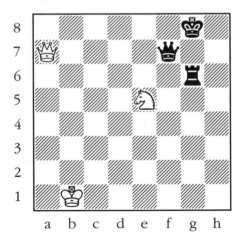

White to Move
135.

White to Move
136.

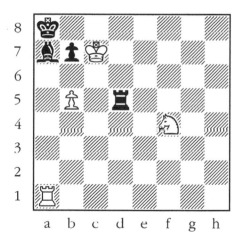

White to Move
137.

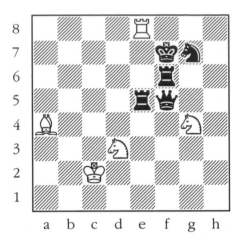

White to Move
138.

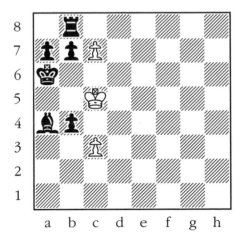

White to Move
139.

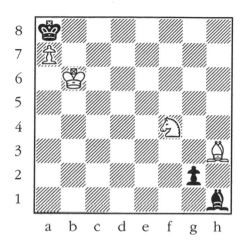

White to Move
140.

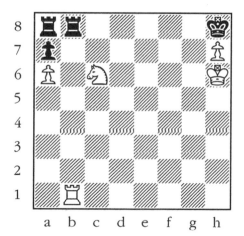

White to Move
141.

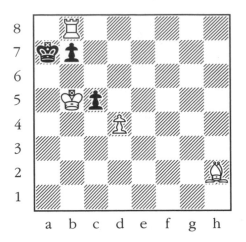

White to Move
142.

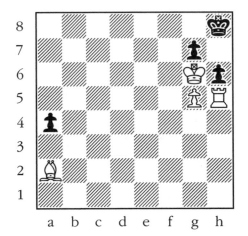

**White to Move
143.**

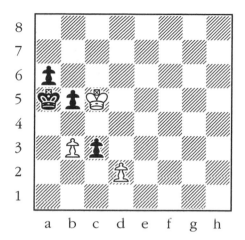

**White to Move
144.**

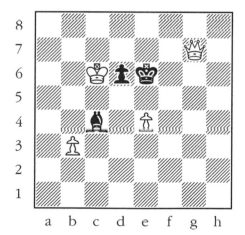

White to Move
145.

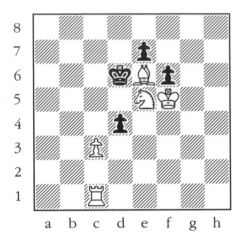

White to Move
146.

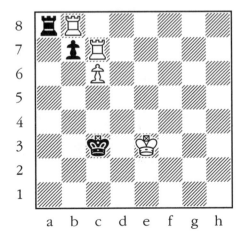

White to Move
147.

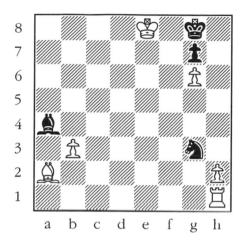

White to Move
148.

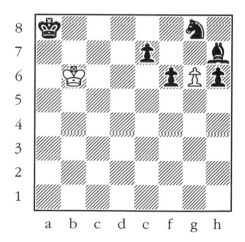

White to Move
149.

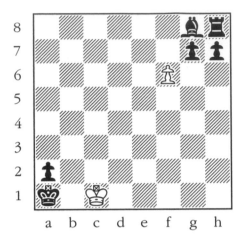

White to Move
150.

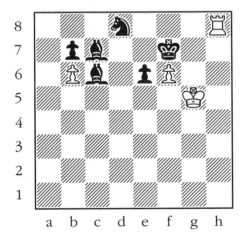

White to Move
151.

White to Move
152.

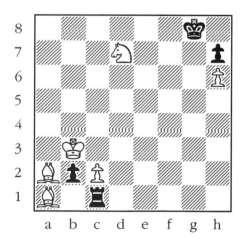

White to Move
153.

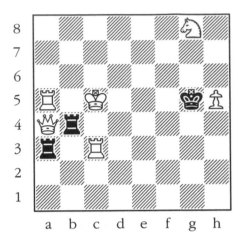

White to Move
154.

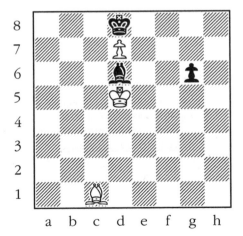

White to Move
155.

White to Move
156.

White to Move
157.

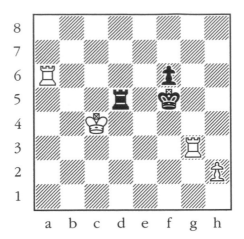

White to Move
158.

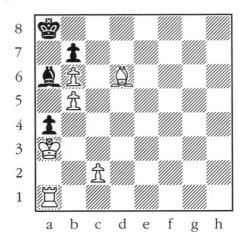

White to Move
159.

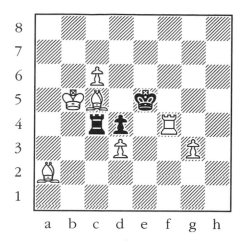

White to Move
160.

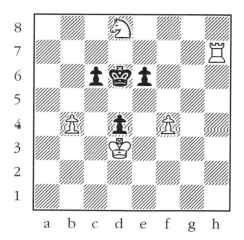

White to Move
161.

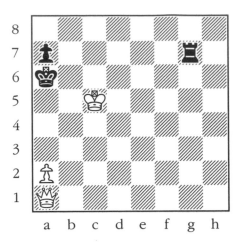

White to Move
162.

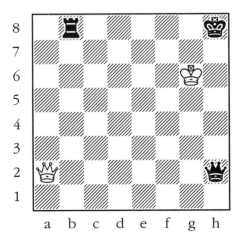

White to Move
163.

White to Move
164.

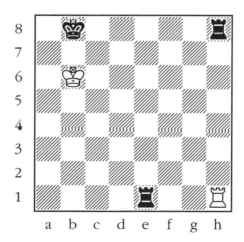

White to Move
165.

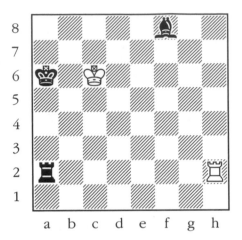

White to Move
166.

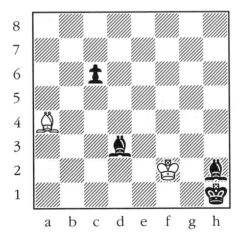

White to Move
167.

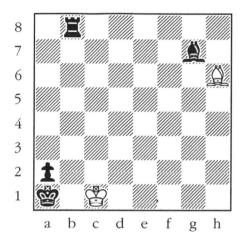

White to Move
168.

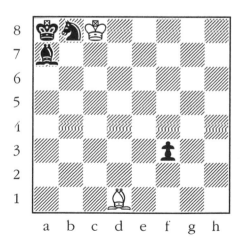

White to Move
169.

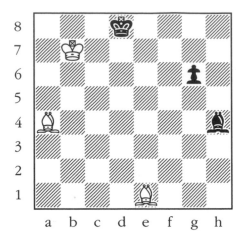

White to Move
170.

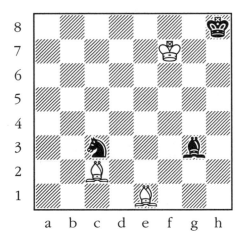

**White to Move
171.**

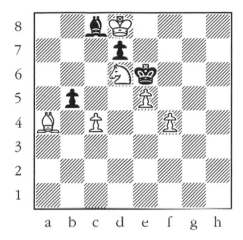

**White to Move
172.**

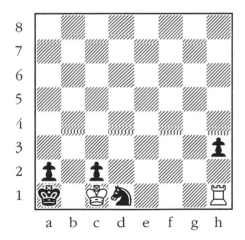

White to Move
173.

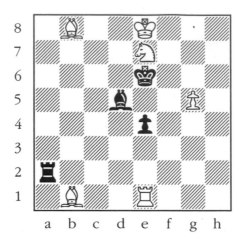

White to Move
174.

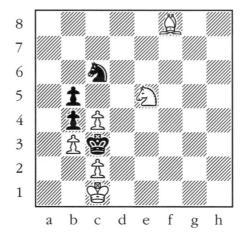

White to Move
175.

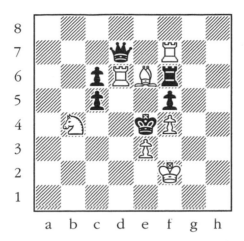

White to Move
176.

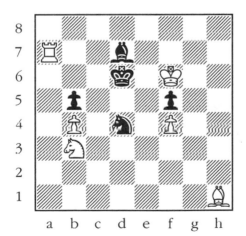

White to Move
177.

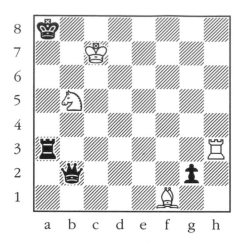

White to Move
178.

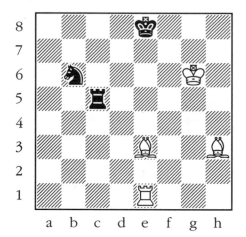

White to Move
179.

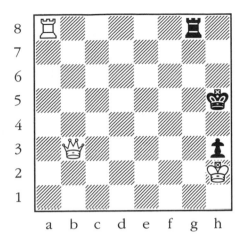

White to Move
180.

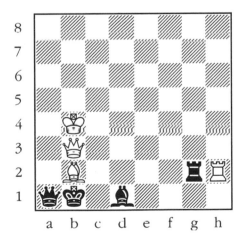

White to Move
181.

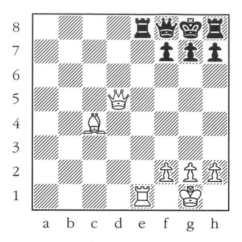

White to Move
182.

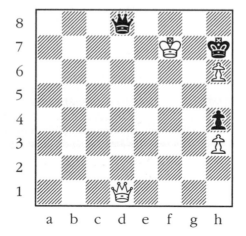

White to Move
183.

White to Move
184.

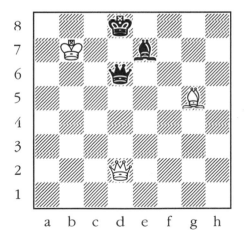

White to Move
185.

White to Move
186.

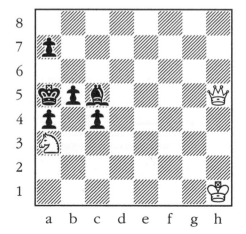

White to Move
187.

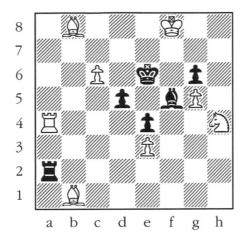

White to Move
188.

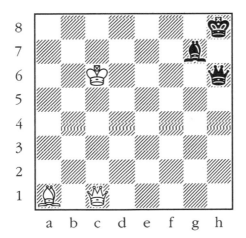

White to Move
189.

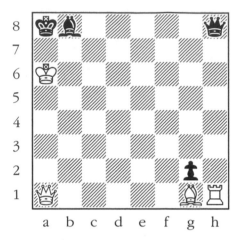

White to Move
190.

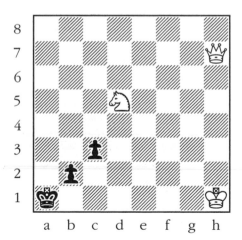

White to Move
191.

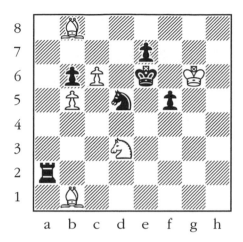

White to Move
192.

White to Move
193.

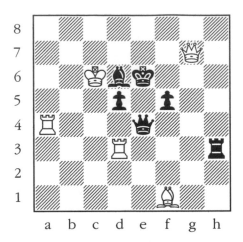

White to Move
194.

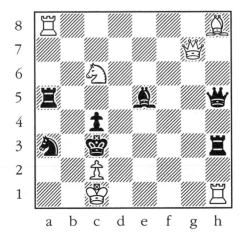

White to Move
195.

White to Move
196.

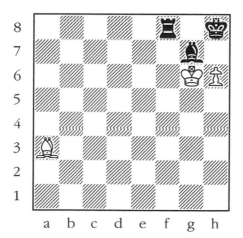

White to Move
197.

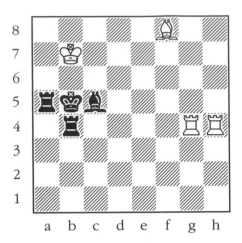

White to Move
198.

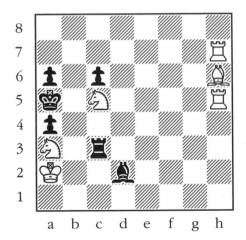

White to Move
199.

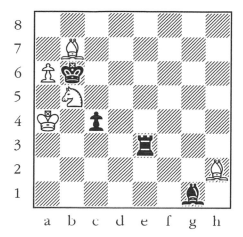

White to Move
200.

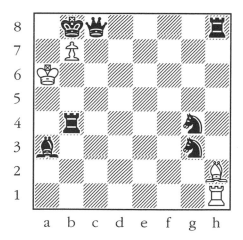

 **Solutions**

Wow! These last two positions were tough! We hope you were able to solve them but, if not, don't stop trying yet.

How about a hint?

Look for a possible "big sacrifice" like the kind we talked about in the introduction. After all, is it possible you give up your strongest piece to force checkmate? We're sure you will find the solutions now!

Okay, now that you have finished going through your first chess workbook what should you do? Well, besides getting some more chess books to study, keep practicing the mates in this book until they are all easy to solve. Remember, "practice makes perfect!"

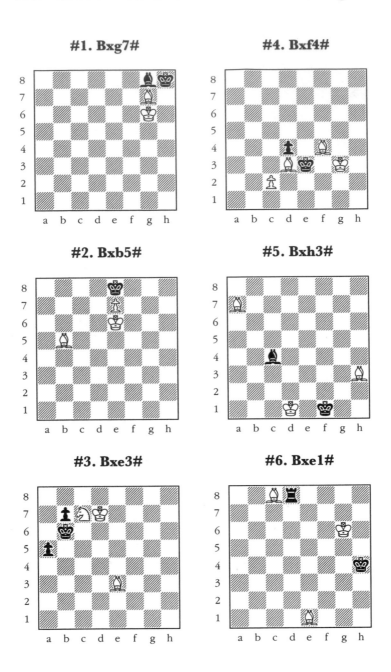

#1. Bxg7#

#4. Bxf4#

#2. Bxb5#

#5. Bxh3#

#3. Bxe3#

#6. Bxe1#

#7. Bxg5#

#10. Rxh1#

#8. Bxb5#

#11. Rexf8#

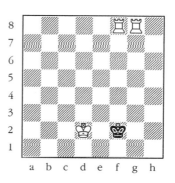

#9. Rxa8#

#12. Rhxh7#

#13. Rxa8#

#16. Rxa4#

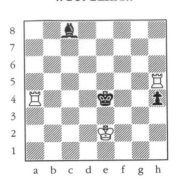

#14. Rxc7#

#17. Qxc8#

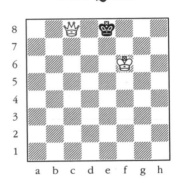

#15. Rxb5#

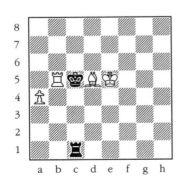

#18. Qxh8#

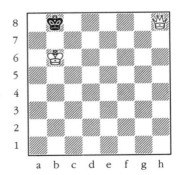

#19. Qxb5#

#22. Qxg6#

#20. Qxa2#

#23. Qxd3#

#21. Qxh7#

#24. Qxe6#

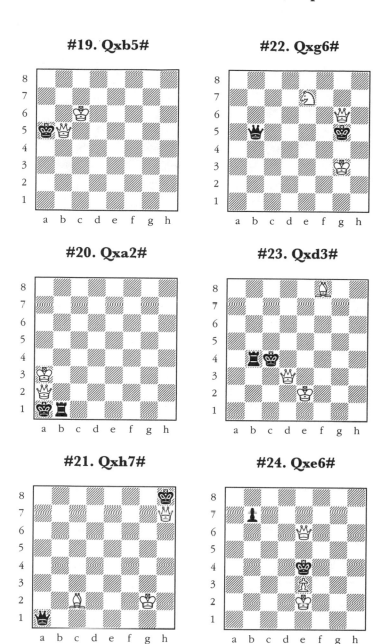

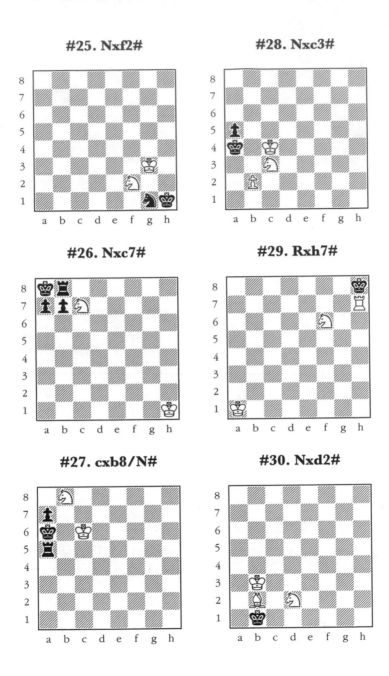

#25. Nxf2#

#28. Nxc3#

#26. Nxc7#

#29. Rxh7#

#27. cxb8/N#

#30. Nxd2#

#31. Nxb6#

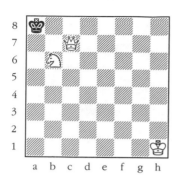

#34. Nxc6#

#32. Nxe6#

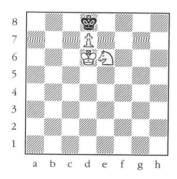

#35. Nxd3#

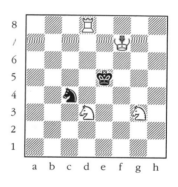

#33. Nxc7#

#36. Nxf6#

#37. Kxf7#

#40. Kxe6#

#38. Kxf2#

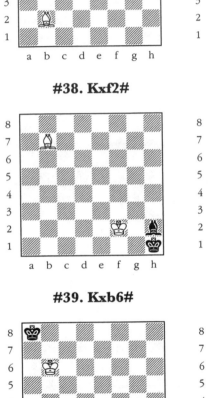

#41. Kxd3#

#39. Kxb6#

#42. Kxd6#

#43. Kxb1#

#46. fxe7#

#44. Kxc6#

#47. cxb5#

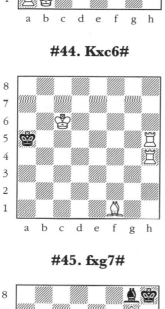
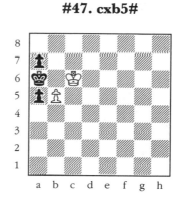

#45. fxg7#

#48. bxc4#

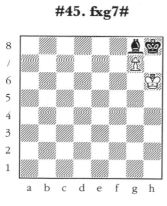
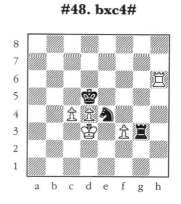

#49. gxh8/Q#

#52. exf8/N#

#50. bxa8/Q#

#53. Bxb1#

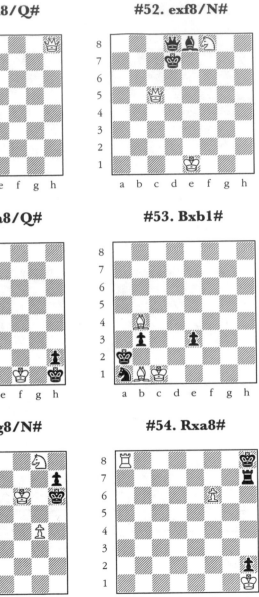

#51. fxg8/N#

#54. Rxa8#

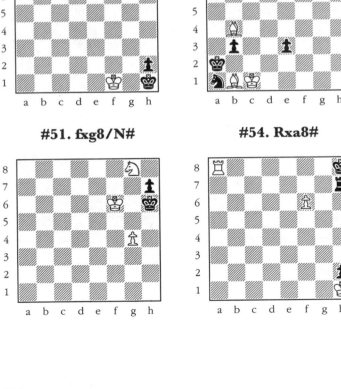

#55. Qxf5#

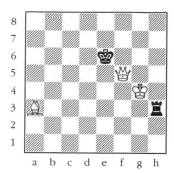

#58. cxd4#

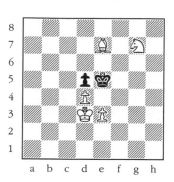

#56. Nxc1#

#59. dxe6#
The *en passant* pawn capture

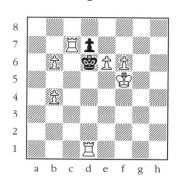

#57. gxh3#

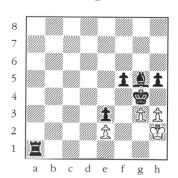

#60. exd5#

#61. Bxb7#

#64. Bxc7#

#62. Bxb7#

#65. Bxg7#

#63. Bxh7#

#66. Bxe3#

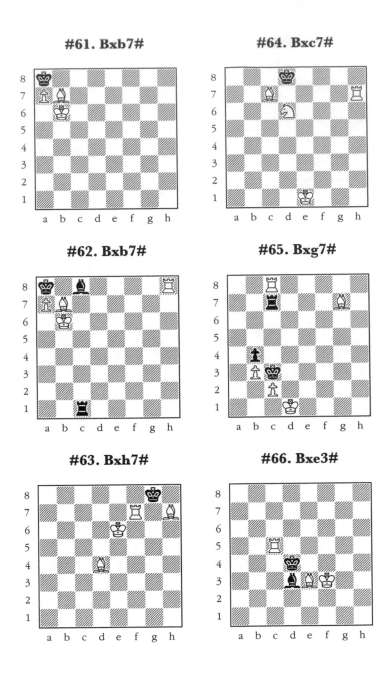

#67. Bxc3#

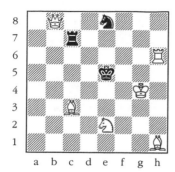

#70. Rxb6#

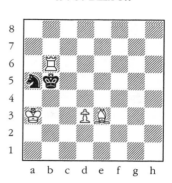

#68. Bxe7#

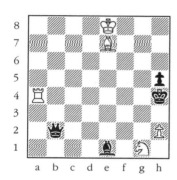

#71. Rxg8#

#69. Rxh8#

#72. Rxd5#

#73. Rxb6#

#76. Rxd4#

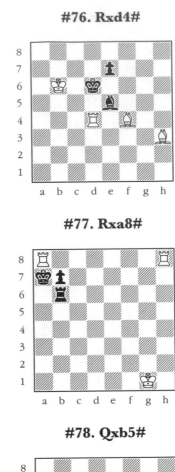

#74. Bxf4#

#77. Rxa8#

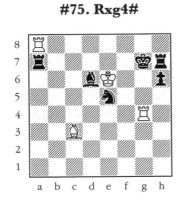

#75. Rxg4#

#78. Qxb5#

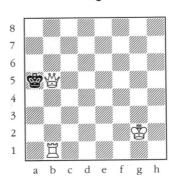

#79. Qxh4#

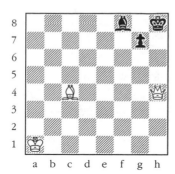

#82. Qxh2#

#80. Rxb8#

#83. Rxf8#

#81. Qxc1#

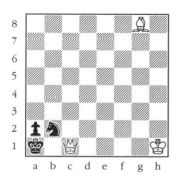

#84. Qxa8#

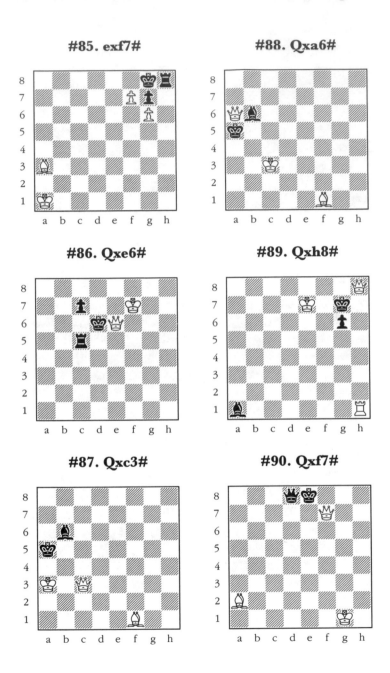

#85. exf7#

#88. Qxa6#

#86. Qxe6#

#89. Qxh8#

#87. Qxc3#

#90. Qxf7#

#91. hxg5#

#94. Nxc7#

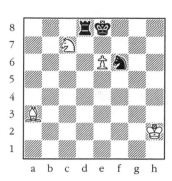

#92. Bxb4#

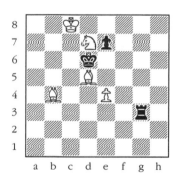

#95. Nxc4#

#93. Nxf7#

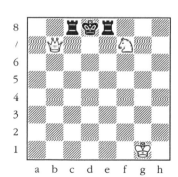

#96. Nxc7#

#97. Bxd5#

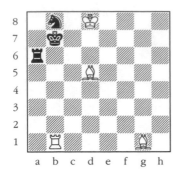

#100. Rxa5#

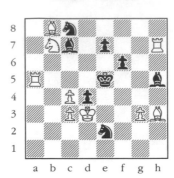

#98. Bxe4#

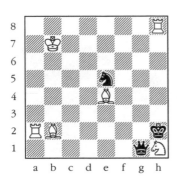

#101. 1. Qxh7+ Kf8
2. Qxf7#

#99. Rxh2#

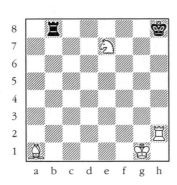

#102. 1.Qxf7+ Kd8
2. Qxd7#

#103. 1. Qxh7+ Kf6
2. Bxe5#

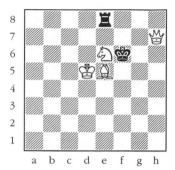

#106. 1. Qxh8+ Rb2
2. Qxb2#

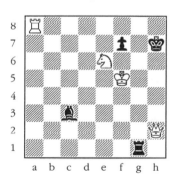

#104. 1. Qxg2+ Ke5
2. Qxg5#

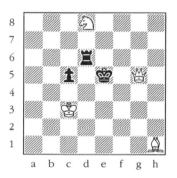

#107. 1. Qxb8+ Kh7
2. Qxh2#

#105. 1. Qxh1+ Kg7
2. Qxh7#

#108. 1. Qxh8+ Kc7(or
1...Ka7 2. Qa8#) 2. Nxa8#

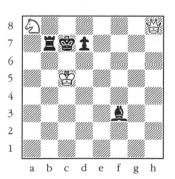

#109. 1. Qxa8+ Kb1
2. Qxa1#

#112. 1.Rxb7 Kf8
2. Rxa8#

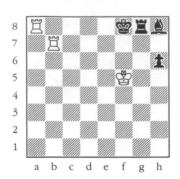

#110. 1.Qxh5+ Rxh5
2. Bxh5#

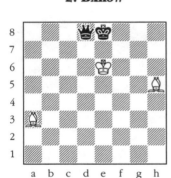

#113. 1.Rxa5+ Kf4
2. Rxh4#

#111. 1.Rxh8+ Ka7
2. Rxa8#

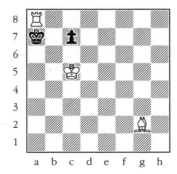

#114. 1.Rxh2+ Ka1
2. Rxa2#

#115. 1.hxg8/R Ka2
2. Rxa8#

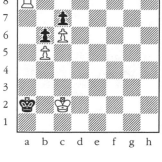

#118. 1.Rxd6+ Kc4
2. dxe5#

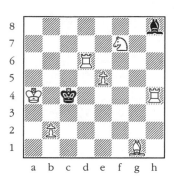

#116. 1.Rbxb5+ Ka4
2. Rxb4#

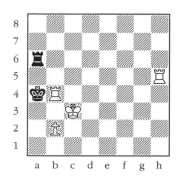

#119. 1.Rxd7+ Ke3
2. Rxd3#

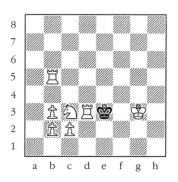

#117. 1.Rxf7+ Kg8
2. Rxg7#

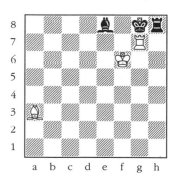

#120. 1.Rxe4+ Kf5[f6] (or
1... Kd5[d6] 2. Rxd4#)
2. Rxf4#

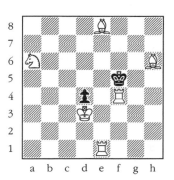

#121. 1.Bxa2+ Kh8
2. Bxf6#

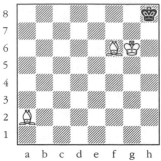

#122. 1. Bxc6+ Kf8
2. Rxe8

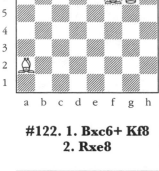

#123. 1. Nxa3+ Ka1
2. Bxg7#

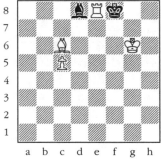

#124. 1.Bxg7+ Ke8[g8]
2. Qxc8#

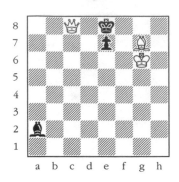

#125. 1.Bxc7+ Kc8[a8]
2. axb7#

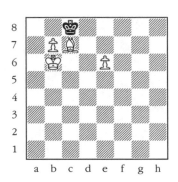

#126. 1.Bxc7+ Kb7[a8]
2. Kxh3#

#127. 1.Kxc3+ Ka5
2. Kxd4#

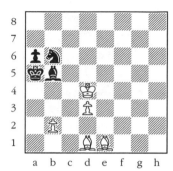

#130. 1. Bxg7+ Kh7
2. Nxg5#

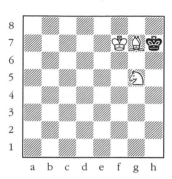

#128. 1.Kxe4+ Kb7
2. Kxe3#

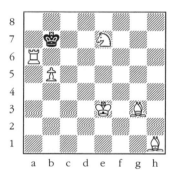

#131. 1. Nxb4+ Ka1
2. Nxb3#

#129. 1.Rxd6+ Kxe5
2. Bxf4#

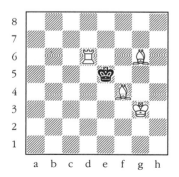

#132. 1.Nxg3+ Kh2
2. Nxf1#

#133. 1.Nxc6+ Kc8[d7]
2. Nxf6#

#136. 1.Nxd5 b6
2. Nxb6#

#134. 1.Qxf7+ Kh8
2. Nxg6#

#137. 1. Ngxe5+ Qxe5
2. Nxe5#

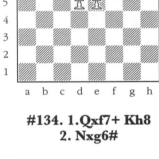

#135. 1.Nxf7+ Kh7
2. Kxe2#

#138. 1. cxb8/N+ Ka5
2. cxb4#

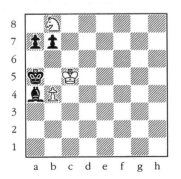

#139. 1. Nxg2 Bxg2 2. Bxg2#

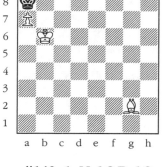

#142. 1. gxh6 a3 (or 1... gxh6 2. Rxh6#) 2. hxg7#

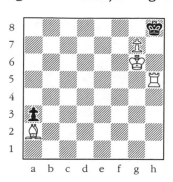

#140. 1. Nxb8 Rxb8 2. Rxb8#

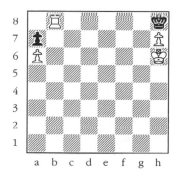

#143. 1. dxc3 b4 2. cxb4#

#141. 1. dxc5 b6 2. cxb6#

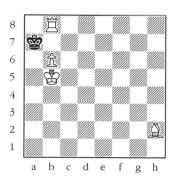

#144. 1. bxc4 d5 2. cxd5#

**#145. 1. cxd4 fxe5
2. dxe5#**

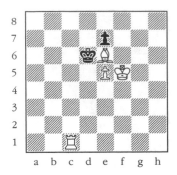

**#148. 1. gxh7 Kb8 (or any
other move) 2. hxg8/Q#**

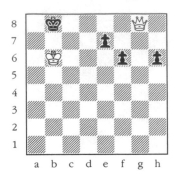

**#146. 1. cxb7+ Kb4[b3,
b2] 2. bxa8/Q#**

**#149. 1. fxg7 h5 (or any
other move) 2. gxh8/Q#**

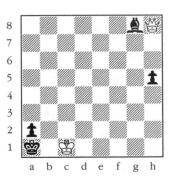

**#147. 1. bxa4+ Kh8
2. hxg3#**

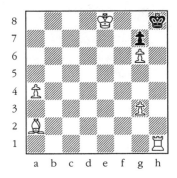

**#150. 1. bxc7 e5 (or any
other move) 2. cxd8/N#**

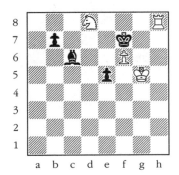

#151. 1.Kxc4+ Ka6
2. Kxb4#

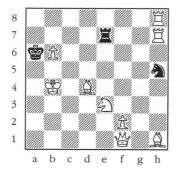

#154. 1. Kxd6 g5
2. Bxg5#

#152. 1. Kxb2+ Kh8
2. Kxc1#

#155. 1. Kxf7 h6
2. Rxh6#

#153. 1. Kxb4+ Kf4[g4,h4]
2. Kxa3#

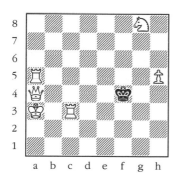

#156. 1. Kxc7 axb6
2. Nxb6#

**#157. 1. Kxd5 Kf4
2. Rxf6#**

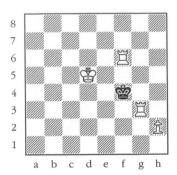

**#160. 1. Kxd4 c5 (or 1...e5
2. fxe5#) 2. bxc5#**

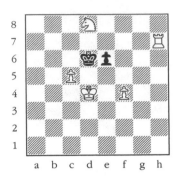

**#158. 1. Kxa4 Bxb5+
2. Kxb5#**

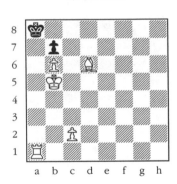

**#161. 1. Qxg7 Ka5
2. Qxa7#**

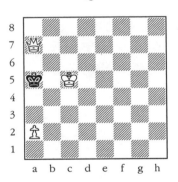

**#159. 1. Kxc4 Ke6
2. Kxd4#**

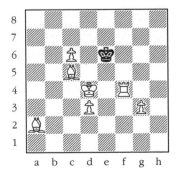

**#162. 1. Qxh2+ Kg8
2. Qxb8#**

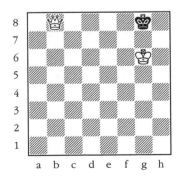

#163. 1. Qxh8+ Bh2+
2. Qxh2#

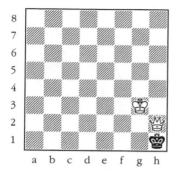

#166. 1. Bxc6+ Be4
2. Bxe4#

#164. 1. Rxh8+ Re8
2. Rxe8#

#167. 1. Bxg7+ Rb2
2. Bxb2#

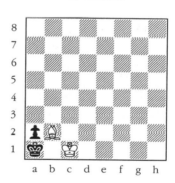

#165. 1. Rxa2+ Ba3
2. Rxa3#

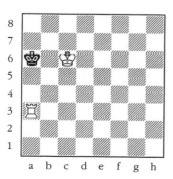

#168. 1. Bxf3+ Nc6
2. Bxc6#

**#169. 1. Bxh4+ g5
2. Bxg5#**

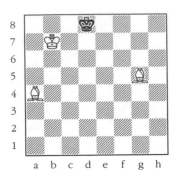

**#170. 1. Bxc3+ Be5
2. Bxe5#**

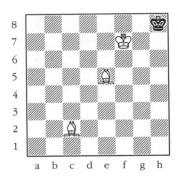

**#171. 1. Bxb5 Ba6[b7]
2. Bxd7#**

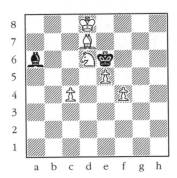

#172. 1. Kxc2 h2 2. Rxd1#

**#173. 1. Bxa2 Bxa2 (or
1...e3 2. Rxe3 or Bxd5#)
2. Rxe4#**

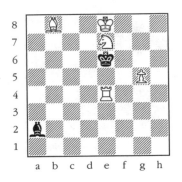

**#174. 1. Nxc6 bxc4
2. Bxb4#**

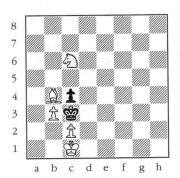

#175. 1. Bxd7 (threat 2. Bxc6#) 1...Rxd6 2. Bxf5#

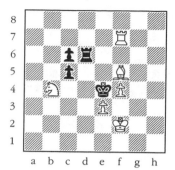

#178. 1. Bxc5+ Kd8 2. Bxb6#

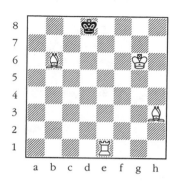

#176. 1. Nxd4 Bc8 (or 1... Be8 2. Nxf5#) 2. Nxb5#

#179. 1. Rxg8 Kh4[h6] 2. Qxh3#

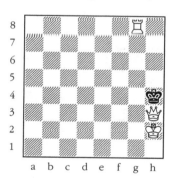

#177. 1.Bxg2+ Qxg2 (or 1...Rf3 2. Bxf3#) 2. Rxa3#

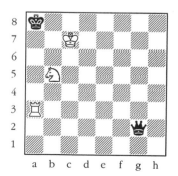

#180. 1. Qxd1+ Kxb2 (or 1...Ka1 2. Qxa1#) 2. Rxg2#

#181 1. Qxf7+ Qxf7
2. Rxe8#

#182. 1. Qxd8 Kxh6
2. Qxh4#

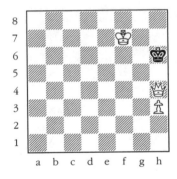

#183. 1. Qxf6+ Ke8
2. Qxe7 #

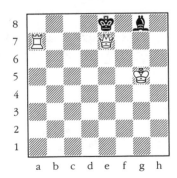

#184 1. Qxd6+ Ke8
2. Qxe7#

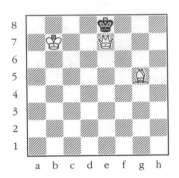

#185. 1. Nxh6 Rg8
2. Qxg8#

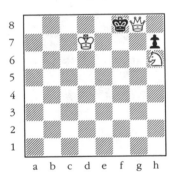

#186. 1. Qxc5 a6 (else 2. Qxb5#) 2. Nxc4#

#187. 1. Bxa2 Bg4[h3]
2. Rxe4#

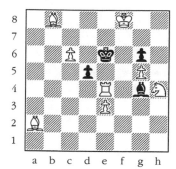

#190. 1. Nxc3 b1/Q+
2. Qxb1#

#188. 1. Qxh6+ Kg8
2. Qxg7#

#191. 1. Bxa2 f4
2. Nxf4#

#189. 1. Qxh8 gxh1/Q
2. Qxh1#

#192. 1. Rxf2 gxf2
2. Bxf2#

**#193. 1. Rxe4+ dxe4 (1...
fxe4 2. Bxh3#; 1...Be5
2. Rxe5#) 2. Rxd6#**

**#196. 1. hxg7+ Kg8
2. gxf8/Q#**

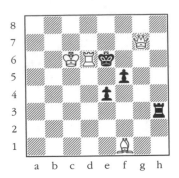

**#194. 1. Qxe5+ Qxe5 (or
1...Rxe5 2. Rxa3#) 2. Rxh3#**

**#197. 1. Rxb4+Bxb4
2. Rxb4#**

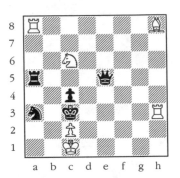

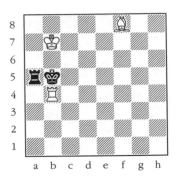

**#195. 1. Rxh8+ Ka7
2. Rxa8#**

**#198. 1. Bxd2 Kb6 (or 1...
Kb4 2. Nxa6#) 2. Nxa4#**

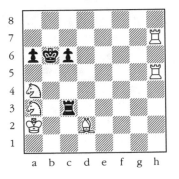

#199. 1. Bxg1 Kc5 (1...c3)
2. Bxe3#

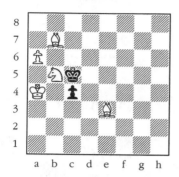

#200. 1. Bxg3+ Rf4 2.
Bxf4+ Ne5 3. Bxe5+ Bd6
4. Bxd6+ Qc7 5. Rxh8#

(The computer slipped in a five-mover when we weren't looking!)